PETER PORTER AFTER MARTIAL

PETER PORTER
AFTER MARTIAL

LONDON
OXFORD UNIVERSITY PRESS
1972

Oxford University Press, Ely House, London W.1

GLASGOW NEW YORK TORONTO MELBOURNE WELLINGTON
CAPE TOWN IBADAN NAIROBI DAR ES SALAAM LUSAKA ADDIS ABABA
DELHI BOMBAY CALCUTTA MADRAS KARACHI LAHORE DACCA
KUALA LUMPUR SINGAPORE HONG KONG TOKYO

ISBN 0 19 211814 5

© *Oxford University Press* 1972

PRINTED IN GREAT BRITAIN
BY THE BOWERING PRESS PLYMOUTH

For Julian Cooper

CONTENTS

INTRODUCTION

Translation is a growth area of modern poetry, and contributing another book of translations requires some apology at the outset, if the charge of pollution is to be avoided. The first objection to translation is that it is impossible: this may also be its justification. However closely a poet keeps to the original, he will still be writing *imitations*, though there are serious points of decorum to be observed in these. Translating the classics is, however, less open to doubt than reworking poems from unfamiliar European languages, such as Russian, Hungarian, and Czech. The Latin and Greek poets have been read by Europeans for two thousand years. Not only are their poems well known, both in the original and in many different vernacular versions, but their influence has moulded our own attitude to poetry and even to our own tongue. So there is no danger that the public will get to know a poet in just one version, which may or may not be an accurate recreation of his intent.

By corollary, this very familiarity tempts each generation (or at least each half-century) to remake the Classics in its own image. I have seen this attitude, in its latest declension, pilloried as 'Sophocles' *Antigone* in English translation, with colour slides of the Parthenon'. There is some truth in this, yet I suspect that even the man of letters with more than a little Latin and Greek savours his own tongue more. Why else did classicists from Harington and Chapman to Dryden and Pope bother with translations from Homer, Virgil, and their peers? Also, English has no verse forms in common with Latin and Greek, and classical poetry has a special strangeness which needs to be naturalized. This need does not arise to the same extent with modern European languages, with which we share a number of forms. The great Augustans put the Classics into heroic couplets, which are remarkable for their fidelity to the tone and subject matter of the originals, but do not resemble them in shape to the slightest extent. (To amplify my contention that English and the dead languages have no verse forms in common, I shall have to throw doubt on such things as English hexameters. Where they exist at all—and

Clough's, for instance, are pretty rough-and-ready—they are parody-forms. The learned men who put Martial into English imitations of Latin elegiacs were forced to write badly—what they were doing was so unnatural. The crux of the matter is that Latin and Greek are quantitative and English qualitative. This makes all the difference, even if you discount rhyme and include such latter-day modes as free verse and syllabics.) One further reason why new versions of the Classics are less questionable than translations of modern poems is that distortions can be seen for what they are, and laid at the door of the translator, not the original author. Good scholars often make bad translators, since they feel no pressing need to render into their own language what they understand and love already. Nevertheless, they should not always ascribe mis-readings to ignorance. The translator's first loyalty is to the poem in English: otherwise, he might as well leave it where it is. Dealing with the Classics, he can create his poems from the ground up—he need not wear himself out trying to match the verse complexities of some highly inflected language rich in rhymes in his own uninflected, sparsely-rhyming tongue. He is on a better wicket with Martial, dead for two millenia, than with the latest myth-maker from beyond the Carpathians.

I am well aware that these poems based on Martial are very definitely re-writings. Ideally, Nabokov's Purity Principle should apply, and I would like to have satisfied myself by avoiding anachronism and vulgarity. But, as Nabokov's own example of *Eugene Onegin* Englished shows, fidelity can destroy all poetry in the process. I found, while working on Martial, that in order to reproduce in my own mind the *effect* of his poems I had to employ a range of devices which ran from comedians' jokes to sonorous Keatsian cadences. What is always missing is the perfection of form which Martial, though he encompasses the most amazing degree of reality and grotesquerie, never fails to achieve. To have tried to approximate to this formality in English with one or two arbitrarily chosen methods—say an insistence on rhyme or an e. e. cummings-like bag of tricks and ampersands—would have been self-defeating. Three-quarters of Martial's epigrams are in

x

elegiacs. No single living English form could have coped with their material and yet matched their concision. Therefore, I tried to find *sui generis* some way of matching each epigram in turn. I have been entirely inconsistent—sometimes rhyming, sometimes using the freest of free verse, often applying devices at whim (there is even one poem which is a concealed sonnet). I discuss in the Notes the deliberate changes I have made in a few of the epigrams: generally, however, I have tried to bring out the point Martial is making faithfully, even if this has led to a greater explicitness and underlining than he found necessary. My worst inconsistency has been my use of anachronism. I have kept most of the Roman proper names and many of the Roman places, but freely set beside them such modern terms and references as serve to explain something *quickly* to the contemporary reader. I quote Mr Burnaby of the Middle Temple, writing at the end of the seventeenth century, as justification of this principle. I was tempted to do what Dudley Fitts does in his book of Martial Epigrams—substitute modern names and instances for the Latin personages and places. He discovers some ingenious equivalents, but I feel that the resulting poems have the wrong tone. My mixed method may be indefensible in theory, but I feel that it works in practice.

Martial has never lacked translators, though only one unobtainable collection includes every one of his poems in English (his obscenity being the reason). The Elizabethans, especially Ben Jonson, loved him, and, in the last century, Robert Louis Stevenson produced some very readable versions. The literal cribs in the Loeb Classics edition, by W. C. A. Ker, are much better than most in that series. And there have been at least a dozen selections produced in the United States, the home of translation-fever. These have varied from the plain (and to my mind pointless) to the ornate and witty. The best are those by Dudley Fitts, which are both skilful and funny, and J. V. Cunningham, whose all-too-few translations are the finest that Martial has ever received, in my opinion. Since he has been so well served, I have tried to choose lesser known epigrams, though such favourites as II. lix; III. xxxv; IV. xliv; V. xxxiv; X. xlvii and XII. xviii are included. What I have avoided are the two-line squibs which are still with us in the Sunday papers—punning rhymes and Christmas cracker jokes which give people a wrong idea of the epigram and of Martial as its greatest exponent. Many of his best epigrams are of considerable length and serious import. He was never pompous but he could be weighty and elegiac. He gives the fullest picture of any poet of antiquity of life as it was then lived, while his observation of human vanity and folly puts him on a par with Jonson, Molière, and Pope. He is amazingly modern, and one does not have to draw apocalyptic parallels between our society and Imperial Rome to feel the force of his satire. Although I have translated the longer epigrams, readers may still feel that I have turned the world's most concise writer into a rather long-winded one. Indeed, only III. xxxv has the same number of words as the Latin. I excuse myself by observing that Latin has a much higher specific gravity than English, and the only way to arrive at the same point as Martial is to forget about economy and go for effectiveness.

Two notorious aspects of his poetry must be mentioned—his obscenity and his adulation of the unspeakable Emperor, Domitian. The latter is truly obscene, but I cannot bring myself to judge a man living at so different a time and in close proximity to such a dangerous court. I have not translated any of his panegyrics, not even on Silius Italicus and Lucan, and none addressed to his disgusting Caesar. The epigrams written for Julius Martialis and Juvenal are not panegyrics but examples of true friendship. However, I have included a disproportionate number of his obscene poems, because I like them and think them the most natural of their kind. About three or four hundred of his more than fifteen hundred epigrams are very dirty indeed, and of this number there are fewer failures than in the clean part of his output. A poem like XI. civ is a *tour-de-force* of heartlessness, but extremely funny and truthful at the same time. I think it pusillanimous of translators to publish selections from the best bawdy poet who ever lived and to exclude entirely the hard core of his obscenity from their books. Having decided to render the more outrageous poems, I had no intention of finding euphemisms for the direct

Latin words used by Martial. Even so, I have not been as straight-forward as Martial himself, and anyone who finds some of these English versions objectionable should look again at the originals. The Loeb edition renders all the really obscene poems in Italian, where dashes and euphemisms won't suffice. I don't believe that my translations will offend anyone, but if they do, I cannot pro-tect myself with the cry that I am telling the truth. Martial ob-served the world sharply, but there is little morality in his censure of it. The absurdity of sexual behaviour and its funny side appealed to him. There are enough sensual poems to suggest that he had no moral objection to the things he poked fun at. It was the decep-tion in people's sex lives he disapproved of, and so he derides their hypocrisy, not their practices. Lastly, in this age of hand-books on sex, especially oral sex, Martial's preoccupations will not be strange. If only our writers, both the censorious and the emancipated, had a quarter of his wit and vivacity.

I don't want to say much about Martial's life or his relationship to his contemporaries. He was a professional man-of-letters and no doubt his life was as uneventful as most such men's are. He was born, probably about AD 40, in the town of Bilbilis, in His-pania Terraconensis, not far from modern Barcelona. His parents (see epigram V. xxxiv) were presumably Roman colonists or fully Romanized, since they gave him a good education. He refers a number of times to his home town: it stood on the River Salo and was famous for producing good quality iron. Martial came to Rome when he was about twenty and stayed there until almost the turn of the century, returning to Bilbilis to settle in a comfort-able house given him by a Spanish lady, Marcella (XII. xxxi). He died there probably around AD 104. He may never have mar-ried; XI. civ, which apostrophizes a wife, sounds more like a character-piece than a personal document. He sought out the most distinguished of his fellow-Spaniards in Rome and enjoyed some support from Quintilian and Seneca early in his life. He speaks well of his Spanish predecessor Lucan. Later, he enjoyed the patronage of the Younger Pliny. He established himself as a successful writer fairly quickly, and became one of the most important literary figures in the capital. He mentions all the best-known poets of his time, with the exception of Statius. His friendship with his younger contemporary Juvenal is well-known, and though he was a much more genial man than Juvenal, their satiric temperaments must have made them obvious allies. His fame, which as early as I. ii, he speaks of as 'world-wide', would not have guaranteed him a decent living, and there are many poems which speak ruefully of his poverty. Some of these may have been tropes to soften the hearts of patrons, but Martial's life must have been a hard one, since his dependence on the public was total. He got to know life in the Imperial city the hard way, which is fortunate for posterity, as also is his need to publish a lot. I doubt that you can infer a poet's character from his writings, but Martial appears to have been warm-hearted and generous, though feared for his wit. It is his unique achievement to have almost vanished as a personality, substituting for himself a detailed picture of the civilization he lived in.

Finally, I hope this book earns the tolerance of scholars, though it is not intended for them. I first began to attempt translation of Martial when reading him for pleasure: I discovered I had an unconscious desire to create the poems afresh in my own mind. This meant remodelling them in English. I have found at many poetry readings that his special cast of mind is still relished by audiences. His poems have suffered a sea-change from their Latin precision in this book, but the man who first conceived them is certainly not remote from modern sensibility.

Four of the fifty epigrams were originally published in my *Poems Ancient and Modern*, by Scorpion Press in 1964. I wish to thank Scorpion for permission to reprint them here. Another eleven epigrams are taken from *The Last of England*, published by OUP in 1970. Some others were in recent issues of *Delos* and *Agenda*.

If I have alter'd or added to the Author, it was either to render those Customs of the Romans that were analagous to ours, by what was more familiar to us, or to prevent a Note by enlarging on others where I found 'em.

From Burnaby's Preface to his translation of the Satyricon.

II. lxxxvi

Because I don't attempt those modern poems
like lost papyri or Black Mountain Lyrics
stuffed with Court House Records, *non sequiturs*,
and advice on fishing; and since my lines
don't pun with mild obscenities in
the *Sunday Times*; nor yet ape Ezra's men
in spavined epics of the Scythian Marsh,
The Florentine Banking Scene, or hip-baths
in Northumberland; nor am I well-fledged
in the East European Translation Market,
whose bloody fables tickle liberal tongues;
despite this I make my claim to be a poet.
I'm even serious—you don't ask a runner
to try the high-jump, and if my trade is words
I'd be a misfit in the People Show.
From Liverpool to San Francisco, poets
are tuning to the Underground, a pop-
ulous place where laurels pale. My pleasure
is to please myself and if the Muses listen
I may find an ear or two to echo in.

I. xliii

What a host you are, Mancinus;
there we were, all sixty of us,
last night, decently invited guests
and this was the order of dishes
you pampered us with:
> NO late-gathered grapes
> NO apples sweet as honeycomb
> NO ponderous ripe pears lashed to the branch
> NO pomegranates the colour of blowing roses
> NO baskets of best Sassina cheese
> NO Picenian jars of olives

Only a miserable boar so small
a dwarf could have throttled it
one-handed. And nothing to follow,
no dessert, no sweet, no pudding, nothing . . .

> We were the spectres, this was the feast,
> a boar fit for the arena, duly
> masticated by us—

> I don't want to see you struggle
> in your turn for a share of the crackling—
> no, imitate instead
> that poor devil Charidemus
> who was shredded in the ring—
> rather than miser eats boar
> let's have boar eats miser:
> *bon appétit*, my host of nothings,
> I can almost feel the tushes in your throat.

I. lxxi

Here's a toast to the ladies—
six tiltings of the jug
To Laevia, seven for Justina,
five for Lycas, four Lyde
and three for Ida: one for
each letter of our mistress' names—
too bad the bitches never come,
so five up-endings of
Falernian more—that'll be enough
to call the girl who never fails,
warm-tailed and celerious sleep!

II. xvii

At the entrance to the dark Subura
    where you catch a glimpse of
the executioners' masterpieces,
    blood-stained bodies hanging
in their beaten racks; where many a cobbler
    knocks out the rhythms of the Potters'
Field—there, Ammianus, sits a famous
    female barber. I said a female barber
but she shears no heads—not for her
    the basin cut, the pudding crop.
What does she do, this female barber,
    if she doesn't clip into a dish?
And why do men flock to her? She won't
    carve or slice you but she'll plate you.

II. lii

Dasius, chucker-out
at the Turkish Baths,
is a shrewd assessor;
when he saw big-titted
Spatale coming, he decided
to charge her entry for three
persons. What did she do?
Paid with pride of course.

II. lix

Small and select, the restaurant called *The Mouthful*
    Overlooks Caesar's tomb and you may view
The sacred domes with garlic on your breath.
    Wine and dine there if you've got the pull,
See and be seen, for even as you chew,
    The God Augustus welcomes you to death.

II. lxx

Our fastidious friend Cotilus is not fond
    of the public baths. You've no idea,
my dear, who's been in before you,
    he says, and lets his face wrinkle up
at the prospect of unnamed pollution.
    I don't mind, if I can be sure
I'm the first, he admits, scraping
    a toe along the water's skin.
To make your prophylaxis certain, Cotilus,
    don't wade in, take a running dive
and get your head under before your prick.

III. xi & III. viii

I was silly enough to use your name
    in a recent epigram, Quintus,
and I spoke of your Thais (perhaps as
    a change from Lais)—after all,
I could have chosen Hermione or any
    other name. To make amends,
I've revised the epigram: Book 3, No. 8:
    'Sextus loves Hermione.' 'Which Hermione?'
'Hermione, the one-eyed.' 'Hermione lacks
    one eye, but Sextus both!' Now the names
are changed, you won't see any similarities.
    Didn't a satirist say that satire
is a sort of glass, wherein beholders do
    generally discover everybody's face
but their own? Names are another matter!

III. xii

At dinner yesterday the smell was heaven
As we sat down to dine at seven;
Fabullus, our host, splashed the place with perfume,
More like a boudoir than a dining room,
But when it came to time to carve
He just sniffed the air and let us starve.
Fabullus, I said, please mind my seat,
I'm off to buy a winding sheet—
To be anointed but unable to ingest
Is the fate of a corpse, not of a guest.

III. xxii

Twice thirty million sesterces spent
In the service of his famous stomach
Apicius followed where his money went
Under a wide and grassy hummock.

He'd counted his wealth and found there were
Ten million left. Mere hunger and thirst!
Soon life would be more than he could bear
So he drank a beaker of poison first.

Romans are noble in everything—yes,
Even Apicius, the notorious glutton.
He died for his principles—to eat the best
And deny the very existence of mutton.

III. xxxv

Instant Fish
by Phidias!
Add water
and they swim.

IV. xviii

Near the Vipsanian columns where the aqueduct
   drips down the side of its dark arch,
the stone is a green and pulsing velvet
   and the air is powdered with sweat
from the invisible faucet: there winter
   shaped a dagger of ice, waited till
a boy looked up at the quondam stalactites,
   threw it like a gimlet through his throat
and as in a murder in a paperback the clever
   weapon melted away in its own hole. Where
have blood and water flowed before from one wound?
   The story is trivial and the instance holy—
what portion of power has violent fortune
   ever surrendered, what degraded circumstance
will she refuse? Death is everywhere
   if water, the life-giving element,
will descend to cutting throats.

IV. xxi

'The skies are empty
  and the gods are dead',
says Segius, the proof of which
is that he sees himself made rich.

IV. xliv

Hear the testament of death:
yesterday beneath Vesuvius' side
the grape ripened in green shade,
the dripping vats with their viny tide
squatted on hill turf: Bacchus
loved this land more than fertile Nysa:
here the satyrs ran, this was Venus' home.
sweeter to her than Lacaedemon
or the rocks of foam-framed Cyprus.
One city now in ashes the great name
of Hercules once blessed, one other
to the salty sea was manacled.
All is cold silver, all fused in death
murdered by the fire of Heaven. Even
the Gods repent this faculty,
that power of death which may not be recalled.

Believe me, Flaccus, the epigram is more
than just a cracker-motto or an inch
of frivolous joking to fill up a column.
Really, he's more frivolous who thinks poetry
demands portentousness, that some subjects
are proper to the Muse and others aren't.
It depends, my friend, which Muse you honour—
you won't get all the usual stuff from me:
Tereus the Terrible eating filial pie,
Thyestes choking over knucklebone soup,
Daedalus fitting out his son with Wool-
worth wings, nor those old scenes from the Odyssey,
especially Brobdingnagian Polyphemus
and his silly sheep. Some call this grandeur
and some tradition; I think it's merely *wind*.
It's tragic only that the Tragic Muse
has to put up with such stilted nonsense.
'What's that you say, everybody likes it,
buys it, praises it. That's what poetry's about,
solemn Horror Stories from the Ancient Greek.'
No doubt, but don't set store by what men praise
nor what they proudly put upon their shelves—
surprise them reading, it'll be something
true and scabrous from my kind of book.

As you know, Regulus, men are pharisaical,
They're always whoring after the classical;
They read but never praise our living writers
(Though the classics hit them like St. Vitus).
For them the time's always out of joint
And the past, being past, can't disappoint.
How they claim they miss those shady halls
Of Pompey's; or despite the balls—
Up Catulus made of the restoration
Of Jupiter's temple for a grateful nation,
How the fogies praise it because it was done
Back sometime around the year One;
Remember what Rome read in Virgil's time,
Old Ennius and the primitive sublime;
Go further down in the collective past,
Who thought Homer was going to last
And in that fashionable sump, the theatre,
Who fancied Menander a world beater?
Recall, if you can without apoplexy,
The lifetime of Ovid, so smooth and sexy,
The greatest Roman stylist only read
By Corinna, his mistress, and then in bed.
Such Injustice! but hang on a second,
Is that Fame, that creature that beckoned,
With slatted sides and a charnel breath
And a club badge saying *Kiss Me Death*?
Then wait a while, my books, I'll stay
Alive and unknown another day—
If I can't be famous till I'm dead
I'm in no great hurry to be read.

V. xviii

Comes December and the giving season, when
every shop is stocked with gadgets—hand-
kerchiefs with Aunts' initials, silly spoons
to lock away forever, candles sculptured
like ten castles, personalized mauve paper
with embossed addresses, and amazing plums
that only Fortnum's would import; why have I
sent nothing better than my own new poems
(home-made nourishment indeed)—am I
self-satisfied or merely stingy? My thoughts
aren't pendulums to swing back all my way—
Great gifts are guiles and look for gifts again;
My trifles come as treasures from my mind.
I quote. To catch the greedy bream you cast
the glittering fly. Which of us hasn't ex-
pectations of his benefactors as
his gods? In truth, the poor man, Quintianus,
is generous to his well-heeled friend when he
looks him out a keepsake, writes a card,
and leaves him off his Christmas Shopping List!

To you, the shades of my begetters, Fronto
and Flaccilla, where you lie in sweet
decay, I commend with love the body
of my darling child Erotion.
                                    A home-
bred slave yet tender as a golden dormouse,
rarer than the Phoenix, whiter than
an unsmudged lily—
                         guide her spirit home
so she may look for lights in Tartarus
and miss the snapping jaws of hell-hound
Cerberus. She'd have lived six shivering winters
if she hadn't died that many days before
the anniversary.
                     Now let her play
light-heartedly in the ever-darkened house
beside such sure protectors.
                                    May my name
be burbling on her tongue, the childish gift
of sorrow spent on age.
                              And monumental earth,
draw back eternal weight from her
small bones;
                   don't be severe and tread
on her with gravity: she never did on you.

V. lviii

Tomorrow is the time to live; tomorrow
   the tide will turn, says Postumus,
the golden days begin. Where's that tomorrow,
   Postumus, when will it arrive?
When it comes, won't it come as today,
   or is it hidden and must we search for it?
Perhaps the Parthians and Armenians
   have it locked in a sacred Ark;
maybe it's already as old as Priam
   or Nestor, and we'll meet it
coming round the other way. Perhaps it can
   be bought; how much then will it cost?
Tomorrow you will live, is that your
   firm intention? To live today
is already too late: *living*, Postumus,
   is what the wise man did yesterday.

VI. xix

I've got the best counsel in the land,
the trouble is I'm not on a States Secrets Case
but in a civil action over three nanny-goats
stolen by my neighbour, and the judge
has already ruled the case is proven!
Yet my barrister's in full cry; he's
already modulated to the Punic Wars,
the massacre at Cannae, Mithridates
and the poison cup, the Age of Sulla
and Mariuses and Muciuses various
as sea shells. Stop a minute please,
just mention *once* my three nanny-goats!

VI. xxiii

Send your husbands to me, wives, says Lesbia,
    I'll recharge their batteries,
And addresses me jokingly, 'Eveready'.
    Really, Lesbia, it's a disease
With you. One's prick isn't an opera singer
    Following the conductor's finger.

You're willing, I must admit, to play your part;
    What hand may do and lip
Is sweetened with the most unusual words
    But it's just bad generalship
To boast our fight will make the bedsprings rattle
    When your face has already lost the battle.

VI. xxvi

Sotades' head is in the noose.
How come? Who would accuse
so upright and so straight a man?
He's under a different sort of ban—
a pity a chap who's so well-hung
has to rely upon his tongue.

It's good to have a quiver-full of kids, Cinna,
    even these days—
  to hell with the population explosion,
  your little woman's done a great job.
    There's just one matter I'd mention,
    none of them is yours!
Nor your neighbours', nor your friend's,
nor the Elks', nor the Buffaloes', nor the Rotarians',
nor even an overnight hippy's in the sleep-out!
    You can tell this lot were mapped
  on unmade morning beds or sliding mats.
    Here's one with steel-wool hair;
    a gift from Santra the Cook;
    that other with the joke-shop lips
  and nostrils like cut-up avocadoes
is the spitting image of Pannichus the Wrestler
    (I'll bet he was never late for rehearsals);
    If you've ever seen Dama, the Baker's Son,
the original idle apprentice, knobbly, cataracted,
    with the expression of a frozen cod,
then you'll recognize your own third son;
    Number Four's the worst—
  his forehead slopes like a loading chute,
his face is as white as a maggot, he's from an unlikely
    source—your bed-mate Lygdus—so you can
    use him the way you do his father,
    it's a hallowed practice!
Consider the one with the coconut head
and ears lie Eeyore, he's a perfect Identikit
of Cyrta the Cretin: two daughters, one dark,
one red-headed, you owe to Crotus the musician,
(some Ball he fluted at!) and Carpus the Bailiff
(it took him quite a time to deliver his injunction!).

If it weren't that
    your other two servants, Coresus, and Dindymus,
        are eunuchs,
you'd be the Niobe of the Age. That's good luck, anyway,
Cinna. The gods won't punish, they'll only pity you.

VI. xl

Lycóris darling, once I burned for you.
Today Glýcera heats me like a stew.
She's what you were then but are not now—
a change of name requires no change of vow.

VI. xlvii

In sickness the world has double purity;
with death so close a cold transparency
descends upon the skin of life; the stream
that snakes as quickly as a dream
beneath the house of Stella and concurs
with jewelled halls and chalcedony doors,
this is no local freshet, for it springs
from Aricia, sipping place of kings;
solemn Egeria set it flowing, Numa
was often there when troubled by a tumour,
Diana of the Crossways' Water-Course,
sacred to the Ninth Italian Muse.
So, pale-boned nymph, your Marcus here complies
with his sickness-vow to offer sacrifice—
a sucking pig that sniffs your garden borders—
I drank your water against doctor's orders
and I'm much better: pardon me my fault,
may dam or upland never give you halt,
instead your crystal waters always slake
my living thirst. The world is warm, opaque,
but death sees through, so one transparent slave
begs of his nymph her light and curing wave—
I watch the crust of earth returning to
its salutary self and drink to you!

VI. xlix

I am not made of fragile elm
and though I wear a fluted helm
I always stand with rigid shaft
however deep or fierce the draught!
My sappy life is given dress
in carvings of long-lived cypress—
a thousand days within my sight
are one tired moon and one bright night,
and like the rose that roots in clay
I live to shoot another day.
Then all who come here out of bounds,
be warned that these are sacred grounds,
just lay a hand on plant or house
and I who guard as well as rouse
will punish the offender where
my kingdom stops by half a hair.
Take note, I am Priapus who
engenders love and virtue too;
my punishments in clusters come,
I plant ripe figs inside your bum
and every thief who jails avoid
shall bear my crop of haemorrhoids.

VI. lxvi

Black, I'll grant you the times we live in. Here's an example,
not even the Government Market where the slaves of nubile years
are auctioned off at a rattle is free of the huckster's ginger:
it's Gellienus I'm speaking of, the People's Auctioneer;
he had a girl whom most knew was not of wholesome savour,
a sort of famished Bunny, too often topped and tailed, but
still a bit of a sizzler, sitting demure and cross-legged
in the heat of the Subura. The bidding was going slowly,
too slowly for his comfort, and though the girl looked decent,
Gellienus fancied the customers might be proving reluctant
for fear she was clapped or dirty, so like the Jew in the story,
he grabbed her and kissed her with more than an uncle's slobber,
this bit, that bit, a veritable ordnance survey—
'By God, I've been all over', he shouted to the bidders,
'She's as sound as the National Grid.' Disgusting, of course,
but she had to put up with it, all in the way of business.
These auctioneers! But this was a case of the biter bitten
(or the kisser clipped), all he achieved by the pawing
was a bidder of six hundred sesterces immediately
withdrew his bid. Be warned, you impudent tricksters,
sometimes the proof of the pudding isn't in the eating!

VII. xvii

How bucolic a bibliotheque
where the charmed reader looks out
over raspberry canes
on the encroaching city! If
in these rural stacks there's room
among the heavyweight authors
for the sort of poem which delights
sophisticated Thalia (say a shelf
between the national epics
and the medical encyclopaedias),
then receive these seven modest
books, with the author's latest
emendations (these alone
will enable your heirs to sell them
to a North African University)—
take them, friendly space of
truth and learning, and guard
them well, for by these inconsequential
gifts the world will come
to honour the country library
of Julius Martialis, man
of taste and friend to genius.

VII. xix

This fragment of mere driftwood is holy:
it's part of the first keel to slice
through undiscovered waters. What the sliding doors
of Bosphorus could not crack nor the inky
storms of that Black and well-named sea
subdue lies in the hands of time.
You are worth more to me, piece of wood,
than a ship at anchor. The sea worm
has pitted you, but you have been beyond
the world's edge and yet come home to me.

VIII. xxix
To I.H.

The short poem signals
much suffering suppressed—
like the German Fleet at Scapa Flow,
only the flying pennants show!

Such terseness shames all us
chapter-and-versifiers—
but what's the point, since Fabers took
enough to make another book?

VIII. lxviii

You are king of gentleman-farmers, Entellus,
    Alcinous's orchards pale by yours;
you have destroyed the very Seasons. Your grapes
    sway through brutal Winter in
corybantic clusters: you hold Bacchus himself
    under glass as an ant in amber—
a woman's limbs are outlined thus in silk,
    so shines a sunken pebble in a stream—
you have bent Nature itself to your mind,
    my Lord of Greenhouses, yet I fear
that, when it comes to factory-farming, death
    has the best of ever-bearing crops.

IX. xxxiii

Outside the Baths you hear applause—
Flaccus, you know the likely cause.
Connoisseurs love fine workmanship,
Maron has let his towel slip.

IX. liv

If I had hillside olives to fatten fieldfares
    or Sabine woods strung with gins
to cruelly carry hot bodies from the sky
    or could conduct like lightning
small morsels down on a stick, to walk
    grand garnerer of their flutterings,
crop on crop in my meadows of death:
    then I would send you these in token
of love, that you might bite their flesh
    as it were mine. Alas, my fields are asphalt
and listen only to the songs of starlings,
    the fidgeting of finches. The green
of tapered hedges hides the shrill sparrow,
    here the magpie suffers an air-change
to death's bird, while the banished kite
    haunts open fields, the only free man
in a heritage of dependence. Instead,
    I offer you the imagination of birds
whose hard eye drops on the brown earth
    without pardon: come to the start
of the world, we will deal with things cruelly
    as we have love and an inclination to.

X. xlvi

Matho wants all he says thought smart.
I gave him these hints for a start.

Sometimes to shock them, say what's good.
It won't be easily understood.

Then say what seems an in-between.
They'll wonder what you really mean.

Now say the bad, your gamut's run.
They want a talker and you're one.

X. xlvii

Friend and namesake, genial Martial, life's
happier when you know what happiness is:
money inherited, with no need to work,
property run by experts (yours or your wife's),
Town House properly kitchened and no business worries, family watchdogs, legal quirks.
Hardly ever required to wear a suit,
mind relaxed and body exercised
(nothing done that's just seen to be done),
candour matched by tact; friends by repute
won and all guests good-natured —wise
leavers and warm stayers like the sun;
food that isn't smart or finicky,
not too often drunk or shaking off
dolorous dreams; your appetite for sex
moderate but inventive, nights like sea-
scapes under moonlight, never rough;
don't scare yourself with formulae, like x
equals nought, the schizophrenic quest!
What else is there? Well, two points at least—
wishing change wastes both time and breath,
life's unfair and nothing's for the best,
but having started finish off the feast—
neither dread your last day, nor long for death.

X. lxvi

It's a piece of Theophrastian cheek
    assigning my Theopompos to
the kitchen seven days a week—
    to lean that face above the stew
which launched a thousand kisses is
    as wasteful as the Trojan War—
those sumptuous curls all scorched and frizzed—
    the gods are pushing things too far!
I fancy you in see-through shirt
    sorting a vintage from the rack;
you simper, 'Under all this dirt
    (the poor thing's been upon its back)
lurks a Falernian True Blue,
    just have a sip and be convinced.'
I'd make a Ganymede of you,
    no mere Custodian of Mince,
we'd romp on the Cytherean shore!
    But, frightful thought, what if instead
my instinct's wrong and my little whore
    from the kitchen prove a cook in bed?

XI. xxx

It's just pathetic fallacy, says Doctor Zoilus,
that the most practised liars, lawyers and poets,
should so frequently have bad breath.

Nerves affect us all, old chap, they play hell
with our digestion, and who is more
open to taint than a veteran cocksucker?

XI. xlvii

Why does Lattara keep away from the Baths
where all the pretty women congregate?

So he won't be tempted to fuck them!

Why won't he go where all the high class tarts are—
outside Pompey's Porch or the Temple of Isis?

So he won't be tempted to fuck them!

Why does he cover himself with yellow linament
like an athlete and take cold baths apart from the girls?

So he won't be tempted to fuck them!

Why, when he appears to avoid the whole generation
of women like the plague, is he a known licker of cunts?

So he won't be tempted to fuck them!

XI. xcix

Yours is a classic dilemma, Lesbia;
whenever you get up from your chair
your clothes treat you most indecently.
Tugging and talking, with right hand and left
you try to free the yards of cloth swept
up your fundament. Tears and groans
are raised to Heaven as the imperilled
threads are pulled to safety from
those deadly straits: the huge Symplegades
of your buttocks grip all that pass.
What should you do to avoid such
terrible embarrassment? Ask Uncle Val—
don't get up girl, and don't sit down!

You're my wife and you must fit my ways
Or leave the house: I don't keep fastdays,
Nor do I care how Tatius, Curius, Numa
Acted—founding fathers and consumer
Research heroes don't make me repent—
Sex is sex whichever way it's bent!
I prefer it served up elegantly:
A bladder full of wine's no enemy
To what we want to do (if it lies longer
At the point it makes the pleasure stronger),
But keep to water as you always choose,
Not caring to make love on top of booze,
And see what happens—half-way through your stint
You feel the urge, you disengage and sprint
To the loo, sad-eyed water-spiller, and then
You're back berating the appetites of men.
Another thing, I set no limit to
Love's duration: if before I'm through
Daylight's screaming in the floral pane
I say it's night-time still, so once again!
What's night to you? No night is dark enough
To get a head of steam up, no rough stuff
Keeps away the dragomans of sleep
Nor touch upon your haunches gets love's bleep!
It's bad enough, god knows, that you're inclined
To go to bed at half-past-bloody-nine
In opaque winceyette and cummerbund—
I like a girl that's naked, with her sun
Blazing its circuit for my solar lips
Or playing lost in space to fingertips;
For kissing I make doves my paradigm,
Beak to beak to dribble out the time;
Your sort of kissing is a woolly smother
Offered at breakfast to your old grandmother

And nothing will persuade you, neither words
Nor noises like those Kama Sutra birds,
To use a hand upon my other altar
Or try that *reservatus* style from Malta.
Consider the tradition of the service:
Andromache rode Hector like a war horse
While posted at the bedroom door the Phrygian
Slaves were masturbating (that's religion
For you), and in legendary days,
When heroes lived on earth and not in plays,
On Ithaca the while the Master slept
Penelope's well-instructed fingers kept
Their own appointment. You say that your arsehole
Is not for use, though good Cornelia, soul
Of Rome and glory of our past, reversed
Herself to Gracchus, Julia reimbursed
Her Pompey at the northern postern, and
Brutus's Portia served him contraband,
While long before the gods had Ganymede
To mix their drinks, proud Juno had agreed
To play the pretty boy to Jupiter—
Then why can't I with you, if Him with Her?
The gods and heroes gave all sex its due
But only abstinence will do for you:
I tolerate Lucretia by daylight
But I want Lais in my bed at night.

XII. xvi

Labienus sells three smallholdings
and buys three houseboys—
Labienus still has three smallholdings.

XII. xvii

Here comes Dives, full tilt from the quack,
   hot as curry but won't keep his bed.
He thinks he'd miss something on his back,
   won't trust doctors, treats himself instead.

'Health, friend, what a gift! Listen to my groans,
   each a pedal note of pain. Fever pulls
the stops out—breathing booms in 8ft tone.
   I let the experts fossick in my stools.

I get into my litter, leave the fever up
   with the carriers, still it hots my face.
It dines on mushrooms, loves to sup
   on oysters from Ostia (that little race

of varicose bi-valves which seem to slip
   past your uvula like silk); it dotes on sow's paps
(see Apicius, his tour-de-force), it will sip
   my Setine while I'm measuring up the laps

of dinner guests, it gulps Falernian
   but refuses Caecuban unless
strained through snow water, gentian-
   tinted. Siesta-sung-to or moon-witnessed

by a serenade, wrapped in roses,
   quilted dark with balsam, stretched out
at banquets breathing what patrician noses
   have expelled, darkened under gout

on purple bedding, simmering its sleep,
   each duck's feather like a fluke of lead,
my fever will not leave me, I must keep
   an omen reader, pools of leeches to be bled

by, Galen's textbooks, a hair of death
    to change the shape of living. O friend,
Sickness is ungrateful, I give it breath
    but still it chases me to worms' end.'

My sympathy, poor Dives, I said, but since
    your fever lives so comfortably,
is so well-off, how could you convince
it to migrate? Over what black sea

should it fly if used to breath of musk?
    Can wine-washed pain fraternise with pus?
Would you have it root in bins, chew husks
    or make a home of sores with Lazarus?

Friend to friend, though from so far away,
greetings and happiness dear Juvenal
(malice aforethought, because we need
sharp natural spurs to our communication,
this prognostication), you're likely
at this moment to be tramping round
that speculator's mile, the loud Subura,
where Empire ticks are sucking blood (called rental)
from families and young provincials slink
home at evening clutching half a kipper;
or perhaps feeling the gravel of Diana's
hill under your thin-soled sandals; or then
fording the thresholds of the newly great,
aware of the sweaty draughts convected by
your toga—the big and little Caelian,
the sixpenny rides to newly elevated
broiler kings brooding on Palatine
penthouses: think of me and how you laughed
when I set off for Spain. I'm all right,
I'm a big frog in Bilbilis: many Decembers
spent in Rome find me back among
these unsophisticated craftsmen
of the heights, kneaders of gold and iron,
great auricular nomens if unable
to do much with the subjunctive. I'm lazy
here, a toff, I raise a spade just
to let it fall (the Government stroke we say);
I make friends in Boterdus and Platea
(I give you two whole pentameters
to laugh at these our Celtiberian names).
When I go to sleep, it's not just pausing,
getting back my strength to tackle tough-guy
patrons and insurgent tradesmen, it's real
long, self-indulgent dreaming: huge un-

conscionable sleeps which even ten
o'clock can't founder. It's my post-war credit
for everything that Rome did; when I hear
some simple corporal at our feeble barracks
playing the Last Post on a wooden bugle
I think of all those stupid pushers listening
to bucinas in the Forum, girls on heat
and clever dicks from Thessaly touching
them up, wiping thumbs on blazers.
They can have it. I don't even have
a toga. If Aunt Lucy turns up at the door
with a basket full of cucumbers and lettuce
come to be useful at a lying-in,
I snatch a yard of ticking from the chair,
wrap it round me and play Jugurtha
or Caractacus upright at a Triumph.
They can't tell the difference, so why bother,
it's the man that makes the toga. Here they spend
hours just helping you, they really care
if you can stand the smell of oakwood smoke,
the savour of mosquito repellents.
My bailiff's wife crowns the dying fire
with my breakfast pot; I see her do it
opening half an eye to let the violet
air in, streaming from the upland plain.
My huntsman follows her, such a youth
as would set a dozen pens free-wheeling
in your bugger's land—one of our sycophants
would have him even if it cost as much
as an actor's villa in oiliest Misenum.
This man would be charmed if I
ventured as far as half-way to his rump;
in a grove of holy pines near Rome meeting him
you'd spend every waiting minute tearing
at your nails, and if he didn't come you'd
make from this fermata half a dozen

sub-Horatian odes. Here he's mine and so
I choose to close him only with my eyes.
He feeds my slaves, gathers up my acorns,
carries from snow-swollen Salo
all my washing water and then asks me
whether he should crop his hair. Here Juvenal
we see the seasons swing as never saw
Romans where the Tiber carries bodies:
this is how I live, friend, this is how
I love to live and am prepared to die.

XII. xxxi

This phalanx of pines, these demi-fountains,
this subtle pleaching, this irrigation system
ductile as a vein (water meadows under mountains),
and my twice-blooming roses richer than Paestum's,
the rare herb-garden—even in January, green—
my tame eel that snakes about its pond,
white dovecote outshone by its birds—I've been
a long time coming home and you, my fond
benefactress, dear Marcella, gave all this
to me. A miniature kingdom to do
with as I please. If Nausicaa with a kiss
should offer me her Father's gardens, you
need not worry: to everything that's grown
I give one answer, *I prefer my own.*

XII. xxxiv

I've counted it up and it's thirty-four years
since our friendship began, old comrade Julius!
The sweet and the bitter came swanning together
but pleasure prevailed. If we took from God's bottle
the pebbles dropped in for each day we've been friends,
the black and the white in two piles neatly sorted,
the white would outnumber the black five times over.
It wasn't perfection. To escape all unpleasantness,
all quarrels and heartbreak—have no one for friend,
be a dusty recluse who can sniff out a motive,
a *tabula rasa* no trust ever wrote on!
You wouldn't be let down as I must unwittingly
have let you down often, you wouldn't get fed up
nor bored stiff nor borrowed from. But what of those years when
the heart leaves its harbour and there's no warmth
in any acquaintance? What comfort can caution bring,
what words for despair? Only past happiness fans into fire,
only old friendship will solace old sorrow.

XII. lxxxv

Orthodox to the last, Fabullus,
you make a moral metaphor
to play up your virility:
*The flavour of sodomy comes out
the other end as halitosis.*

This has a heterodox side,
what do you say to another aphorism
for your medical table talk?
*The uxorious man doesn't get his fishy
smell from licking postage stamps.*

XIV. xxxix
A Bedside Light

I show but do not countenance what you do.
Douse me. The only record is in you.

These notes are intended to clarify only a few specific difficulties in the translations. The reader should consult a history of Latin Literature or a study of Roman Life in the first century AD for more general information.

II. lxxxvi This epigram serves as introduction to the book and sounds the keynote of the collection. Hereafter the epigrams are printed in their original sequence. The changes in this one are very great and are meant to help authorial identification. The fashionable modern verse styles substituted for Martial's Sotadics, galliambics, and so on are considerably less scurrilous. The tone of slightly aggrieved traditionalism is in Martial's poem also.

I. xliii The joke of NO before all the choice dishes is imitated from a cartoon in the Russian comic journal *Krokodil*.

II. xvii The Subura was the crowded quarter of Rome, occupied by street markets and tenements—a place avoided by all well-off people unless they were slumming. 'Plate' is modern London slang for oral sex.

III. xi Epigram III. viii is included in the middle of its sequel. The quotation from Swift is supererogatory, but fits nicely.

III. xxii Apicius was a real man and the most notorious glutton (or gourmet according to your choice) in Rome. He exhausted his enormous wealth in pursuit of new culinary delights. Legend says he committed suicide rather than face plain food. A translation of his cookery book was a recent publishing hit.

IV. xliv The eruption of Mt. Vesuvius which destroyed the cities of Pompeii and Herculaneum occurred in AD 79, a few years before Martial began publishing epigrams in Rome. There is a description of the eruption in the Younger Pliny's letters. When Martial wrote this epigram, the memory of the disaster would still have been fresh.

IV. xlix A lot of trouble has been taken to identify the Flaccus whom Martial addresses in a number of epigrams. He was almost certainly a contemporary. On the other hand, some of the names in the epigrams are generic or Theophrastian ones, chosen to point up the appropriate humour or characteristic. The Jacobeans, Restoration playwrights, and English Augustans did the same—either by using self-revealing names derived originally from the old Morality plays, such as Malvolio,

Mistress Overdone, Face, Subtle, Sir Epicure Mammon, Fainall, Marwood, Horner, or names from the classics, such as Chloe, Amaryllis, Strephon. When Martial attacks a man by his proper name, the chances are that he is safely dead. This epigram is a spirited and unepigrammatic defence of the epigram form itself.

V. x   Regulus is a like case to Flaccus, except that he is known for certain. He was an advocate and very wealthy. Like so many successful men in the reigns of Nero and Domitian, he seems to have been unscrupulous. Martial flattered him (this is far the nastiest aspect of Martial's character). The Catulus in the poem is not the poet (he has two l's) but a Consul. It is interesting to observe how firmly fixed the Pantheon of poets was even in Martial's time.

V. xviii   The ritual of exchanging gifts in Rome requires a whole study in itself. There was always the motive of gaining something better in return. Our giving of Christmas presents is our only near-equivalent. The italicized quotation is from the fine anonymous lyric set by John Dowland, *Fine Knacks for Ladies*. It has no business here, but I like the feeling of it. For another poem about gifts (this time with sexual overtones) see, IX. liv.

VI. xxvi   An example of the appropriate sort of name-giving mentioned in the previous note on IV. xlix. The original Sotades was a Greek poet who wrote poems in praise of homosexuality (and other sexual variations), and had a species of erotic poetry named after him. Lemprière remarks laconically that he was executed by Ptolemy Philadelphus by being cast into the sea in a cage of lead. Martial is obviously referring to a real acquaintance to whom he gives the characteristic name of the most notorious poet of antiquity. The poem is a witty specimen of the very thing it mocks.

VI. xxxix   I hope the exuberance of the many anachronisms may go some way towards excusing them. A 'sleep-out' is a harking-back to my Australian youth. It is a covered-in verandah where people sleep in hot weather.

VI. xlvii   I have made very considerable changes in this poem. Whether such a stream ran through the house of the actual Stella, who was friend and patron of Martial, I doubt. Martial's final lines say almost exactly the opposite of what I say.

VI. xlix   Statues of Priapus set in gardens served to protect property from theft or trespass. The punishment promised to offenders was traditional to the god.

44

VII. xvii   Julius Martialis was our Martial's closest friend and a collector of the poet's books. He is also addressed in X. xlvii and XII. xxxiv. Thalia, the Muse of Festivals and Comic Poetry, presided over the composition of epigrams. Martial, who frequently invokes her, calls her 'The Ninth Muse', though the nine sisters do not seem to have had any acknowledged running order.

VII. xix   This could be a piece of the *Argo* itself—or, more likely, a relic of as doubtful an authenticity as most of the contents of Christian reliquaries.

VIII. xxix   Mr. I. H. is this poem's onlie begetter: Faber & Faber are his publishers. Martial, who writes brief poems himself is casting doubt on the fashionable short poem, since enough of them will only go to make another book.

X. lxvi   I have completely altered the ending in order to incorporate the final joke.

XI. xcix   The Symplegades were two rocky islands at the entrance to the Bosphorous which were reputed to clash together and destroy any ship attempting to sail between them.

XI. civ   This is my most self-conscious 'imitation', no other epigram being subjected to such expansion. Lais was as famous for her wantonness as Lucretia for her chastity. Tatius, Curius, and Numa are examples of early Roman morality and fortitude, the sort of Republican hardihood praised by Cato.

XII. xvii   I thought it permissible to substitute the Gospel figures of Dives and Lazarus for Martial's originals, as better known examples of the antinomy of rich and poor.

XII. xviii   Martial's Twelfth Book of Epigrams was sent back to Rome from his retirement in his home town of Bilbilis, Hispania Terraconensis (not far from modern Barcelona). He was evidently given a delightful villa there by his benefactress, Marcella (see XII, xxxi). Juvenal was a younger man by several years, and Martial recalls the hard literary life in Rome by reflecting that Juvenal must still be going through all its annoyances and humiliations. Despite his tone of relaxed retirement, he misses Rome. It's agreeable to think of the friendship which existed between these two men, the last of the great Latin Poets.

XII. xxxi   Paestum was a fashionable town with villas and gardens (it still harbours the best preserved Greek temple in Italy). Nausicaa's father, Alcinous had splendid gardens.

INDEX OF FIRST LINES